CW01590169

Subscribe to New Word A Day!

Email us at:
FeedBack@NewWordADay.com

Get a daily word in your email.
Signup Free at NewWordADay.com.

FORGO

<For-go>

Abandon; quit; decline;

Abstaining from a desired action.

Forgo the donuts and abandon treats and you will win the race.

FOR - GO

For	(Reminds)	Forget
Go	(Reminds)	Go

Memory Trick: We forget and let it go when we quit.

FORGET GO

I will forgo donuts. I will not eat them again.

I serve you peas to appease you.

Why does it not work?

You don't like peas. Appease means to calm or pacify. Something you don't like will not make you happy.

ASSUAGE

<Ah-swayge>

Abate; relieve; soothe;

Making something milder.

It will assuage your chill and warm you.

ASS - UAGE

Ass	(Reminds)	Assist
Uage	(Rhymes)	Away

Memory Trick: Assist your troubles away.

ASSIST AWAY

I see you found a way to assuage your chills.

ABRIDGE

<Ah-bridj>

Abbreviate; truncate; shorten

Condensing something while keeping the general idea.
Abridge the book and it will be half the size because the extra words are removed.

A - BRIDGE

Bridge	(Reminds)	Bridge

Memory Trick: We bridge words by removing the extra words.
BRIDGE

Q: You have punctilious punctuation. What should be done to correct it?

I took the time to abridge my book.

ABROGATE

<Ab-ro-gate>

Abolish; reject; nix;

Mutually agreeing to put an end to something, usually a contract.

We will abrogate the contract because we both agree that it should be ended.

A - BRO - GATE

Bro	(Reminds)	Brother
Gate	(Reminds)	Gate

Memory Trick: We are brothers and agree to close the gate.

BRO GATE

A: Nothing. Punctilious means doing something with great care. Your punctuation is very good.

We will abrogate the contract and end it.

BRUSQUE

<Brusk>

Abrupt; blunt; curt;

Behaving in an unfriendly and direct way.

Your attitude is brusque. Please speak in a more pleasant tone.

BRUSQUE

Brusque	(Reminds)	Brisk or quick

Memory Trick: We speak in a brisk way when we are curt.

BRISK

The brusque robot was blunt and stopped me from talking. It then proceeded to scold me.

You become a sexagenarian. Why can you stay in bed all day?

You are probably retired. A sexagenarian is at least the age of 60 and younger than 70.

PILLORIED

<Pil-lor-reed>

Abuse; contempt; despised;

Ridiculed and punished by a group

The pilloried writers learned their lesson and threw the stories out.

PILLOR - IED

Pillor	(Reminds)	Pillory

Memory Trick: A pillory is used for punishment.

PILLORY

He was pilloried because of the mistake he made. No one liked him.

CONTUMELY

<Kon-toom-lee>

Abuse; scorn; arrogance;

Having contempt or making an insult.

He was rudely treated in a contumely way.

CON - TU - ME - LY

Con	(Reminds)	Con
Tu	(Reminds)	To
Me	(Reminds)	Me

Memory Trick: Con to me when you are insulting.

CON TO ME

Q: I say your fame is ephemeral.

Why do I talk about fifteen minutes?

The contumely woman put her finger in my face and she was very rude.

AGGRANDIZE

<Ah-grand-eyes>

Acclaim; glorify; honor;

Making something bigger than it is.

We aggrandize celebrities by making them larger than life.

AH - GRAND - IZE

Grand	(Reminds)	Grand
Ize	(Reminds)	Eyes

Memory Trick: We make them grand in our eyes.

GRAND EYES

A: I probably mean fifteen minutes of fame. Fifteen minutes of fame is when someone is famous for a short time. Ephemeral means short-lived.

She would always aggrandize people she liked.

LAUDATION

<Law-day-shun>

Accolade; acclaim; glorification;

Praising with a speech.

I will give you a laudation and the crowd will cheer you.

LAUD - ATION

Laud	(Reminds)	Lord or a king
Ation	(Reminds)	Salutation

Memory Trick: Praise for a lord.

LORD SALUTATION

He got a wonderful laudation and everyone cheered.

You wear a fancy hat. You get comments on the inelegance of it. What will you probably do next?

Stop wearing the hat. Inelegance means ungraceful or crude.

ACCRETION

<Ah-kre-shun>

Accumulation; increment; addition;

Gradually grow by an outside source.

Water is an accretion for a beach because creates it from the sand.

ACC - RETION

Acc	(Reminds)	Accumulate
Retion	(Reminds)	Ration

Memory Trick: We accumulate a ration when it grows.

ACCUMULATE RATION

An accretion of sand created my favorite beach.

ACRIMONIOUS

<Ack-kre-moan-ee-us>

Acrid; bitter; caustic;

Having a bitter temper.

You are never acrimonious because you are always happy.

A - CRIM - ONIOUS

Crim	(Reminds)	Crime
Monious	(Reminds)	Harmonious

Memory Trick: It is a crime to not be harmonious.

HARMONIOUS

Q: Your banner has a banal phrase. What kind of phrase is it?

The acrimonious cat was always mean.

OBDURATE

<Ob-jer-rayt>

Adamant; harsh; dogged;

Being stubborn. Being indifferent to advice.

He is obdurate and will not listen to advice because he is not yielding.

OB - DU - RATE

Ob	(Reminds)	Object or refuse
Rate	(Reminds)	Berate

Memory Trick: Object to being berated.

OBJECT BERATE

A: A banal phrase is a common or boring saying. Perhaps it says, "It takes two to tango."

The cat was acting obdurate and stubbornly refused to get off my book.

ANNEX

<An-neks>

Addition; attachment; appendix

Adding an extension to something that already exists.

We added an annex to the building and it added two more rooms.

AN - NEX

Nex	(Reminds)	Next

Memory Trick: Next to something is something new.

NEXT

Q: How many utters does a cow have?

We built a little annex next to the building because we needed an extra room.

EFFICACY

<Ef-fah-ka-see>

Adequacy; effectiveness; potency;

Producing a positive and strong effect.

The efficacy of the medicine was good and I was cured.

EFFIC - ACY

Effic	(Reminds)	Effort
Acy	(Reminds)	Ace or expert

Memory Trick: Effort by an ace is effective.

EFFORT ACE

A: None. Cows can't talk. The meaning of Utter is to talk. Cows have udders.

The efficacy of the coffee was apparent.

NIGH

<Nye>

Adjacent; bordering; near;

Being close or near.

You are nigh to me and I can hear you whisper.

NIGH

Nigh	(Reminds)	Near

Memory Trick: You are near.

NEAR

YOU ARE NIGH AND I CAN
HEAR YOU SIGH.

You give your cat a quibble and a bowl of pasteurized milk. Why is it not eating?

Quibble means to argue. You give your cat an argument. It probably does not feel like eating.

UPBRAID

<Up-brayed>

Admonish; castigate; censure;

Placing blaming or scolding.

You upbraid your dog and it learned its lesson.

UP - BRAID

Up	(Reminds)	Up
Braid	(Reminds)	Bray

Memory Trick: We up and bray as we admonish.

UP BRAYED

I always have to upbraid the cat for sitting on the dog.

QUASI

<Kwa-zeye>

Alike; partly; so-called;

Resembling or being almost alike something.

You are a quasi-teacher because you teach well.

QUA - SI

Qua	(Reminds)	Quack or a fake
Si	(Rhymes)	Sigh

Memory Trick: You are faking, but it works and I sigh.

QUACK SIGH

Q: You walk in the woods. You enjoy the preternatural scenery. Why do you feel funny?

A cat is a quasi tiger.

ENVENOM

<En-ven-nom>

Anger; enrage; infuriate;

Embittering someone with your actions

He will envenom his co-worker by arriving late.

EN - VENOM

Venom	(Reminds)	Venom

Memory Trick: We act with venom and make others mad.

VENOM

A: Preternatural means being unusual. You feel funny because the scenery is unusual and strange.

He found that he would envenom them because he did not share the carrot.

ENNUI

<On-we>

Apathy; melancholy; weariness;

Causing tiredness and boredom.

The music relieved our ennui and we no longer were bored.

EN - NUI

En	(Rhymes)	On
Nui	(Rhymes)	Wee or small

Memory Trick: We are on a wee topic that is boring.

ON WE

Q: We are walking to the dress shop. You trip and I catch you. I say, "You are abreast to me." Why did I say that?

He was so boring an ennui came over the room and we all fell asleep.

WINSOME

<Win-sum>

Appealing; captivating; delightful;

Causing joy or pleasure.

The singer had a winsome voice and the music was delightful.

WIN - SOME

Win	(Reminds)	Win or to gain
Some	(Reminds)	Some or a bunch

Memory Trick: We win some when we are pleased.

WIN SOME

A: We are walking side-by-side.

Abreast means side-by-side.

The winsome boy had a captivating smile.

CODICIL

<Kod-dis-sil>

Appendix; postscript; supplement;

Being an addition that contains more information about a document.

Add a codicil and summarize everything.

CO - DI - CIL

Co	(Reminds)	Combine
Di	(Reminds)	Di or two
Cil	(Reminds)	Sil or a windowsill

Memory Trick: We combine two things and look out the sil.

COMBINE DI SILL

I want to add this codicil before we turn the report in.

We are at the zoo and you are lionized. Your nametag is blank. How do I know who you are?

Lionized means to be treated like a famous person. I know your name because you are famous.

ACCEDE

<Ah-seed>

Approve; concede; yield;

Giving consent and agreement.

I accede because you convinced me to allow you to go to the party.

ACC - EDE

Acc	(Reminds)	Accept
Cede	(Reminds)	Concede

Memory Trick: We accept and concede when we yield.

ACCEPT CONCEDE

Okay! I will accede to your demands and I will feed you.

AMOROUS
<Am-or-us>

Ardent; attracted; romantic;

Lusting after someone.

He is very amorous because she is beautiful.

AMOR - OUS

Amor	(Reminds)	Amour or love
Ous	(Sounds)	Us

Memory Trick: They are amour with us.

AMOUR US

Q: Your dinner is a delicious diminution of a meal. How full are you?

TO BE AMOROUS,
IS A LOVE SO TRUE,
WITH PASSIONATE LUST,
THEY WILL FOLLOW YOU.

EXPOSTULATE

<Ex-potch-chew-late>

Argue; protest; complain;

Reasoning earnestly.

You expostulate with the children and convince them that monsters are not real.

EXPOST - ULATE

Expost	(Reminds)	Expose
Ulate	(Reminds)	You late

Memory Trick: Expose you until I make you late.

EXPOSE YOU LATE

A: You are not full. Diminution means to get smaller. Your meal is smaller.

YOU MUST EXPOSTULATE,
TO EASE ALL THE FEAR,
FOR THEY STAY UP LATE,
AND MONSTERS ARE NEAR.

ABET

<Ah-bet>

Assist; prod; support;

Helping in the carrying out of a plan.

You abet someone when you drive the get-away car while they do the robbery.

A - BET

A	(Reminds)	A
Bet	(Means)	Bet or challenge

Memory Trick: I bet you will help me.

A BET

Q: A denizen comes into the house. You run out. The denizen chases you down the street. What are you?

MONEY YOU MAY GET,
WHEN YOU ABET

MICROSCOPIC

<Mike-cro-scop-ick>

Atomic; minute; teeny;

Something that is too small to see by eye.

Ants are microscopic because we need a magnifier to see them well.

MICROSCOP - IC

Microscop	(Reminds)	Microscope

Memory Trick: A microscope is needed to see it.

MICROSCOPE PICTURE

A: A robber. A denizen is a resident. The person lives there and you do not.

WHEN ANTS
ARE THE
TOPIC,

THEY'RE TOO
SMALL TO
SEE,

THEY'RE SO
MICROSCOPIC,

THEY CAN SNEAK BY ME.

EXPIATE

<Ex-pee-ate>

Atone; amend; absolve;

Seeking forgiveness for a guilty action.

I apologize to you and expiate my guilt.

EX - PIATE

Ex	(Reminds)	Ex or the past
Piate	(Reminds)	Pity

Memory Trick:

It is past and I have pity.

EX PITY

Q: I bring a conundrum. The band stops playing and listens to me. Why does the band look confused?

He asked to expiate his guilt. He was sorry for eating all the cookies.

ZEITGEIST

<Zite-guyst>

Attitude; outlook; characteristic;

Representing the spirit of a time.

The zeitgeist of the decade is hard work and serious pursuits.

ZEIT - GEIST

Zeit	(Rhymes)	Site
Geist	(Reminds)	Ghost or sprit

Memory Trick: The site ghost tells us what the spirit was at the time.

SITE GHOST

A: A conundrum is a riddle. It makes no music. The band is puzzled by my riddle.

The zeitgeist of the time was wearing flowered hats. It lasted until the bees discovered the hats too.

AESTHETIC

<Ah-stet-tik>

Attractive; artistic; cultivated;

Concerned with the appreciation of beauty or good taste.

It was an aesthetic improvement because it made the house more beautiful.

AESTHETIC

Aesthetic	(Reminds)	Artistic

Memory Trick: It is artistic to make pretty improvements.

ARTISTIC

The flowers improved the aesthetic look of the doghouse.

I am incurious about the package. I prod and poke it. It has a maroon ribbon. How fast do I open it?

Not fast at all. Incurious means not being interested.

BRAZEN

<Bray-zen>

Audacious; brash; bold;

Bold without caring about shame.

The brazen seagull stole the fish and we were shocked by its daring.

BRA - ZEN

Bra	(Reminds)	Bray
Zen	(Reminds)	Zen or a high state

Memory Trick: A mule brays and its Zen is bravery.

BRAY ZEN

I LIKE TO BRAY,
BECAUSE I'M BOLD,
I DON'T RUN AWAY,
TRUTH BE TOLD.

ASCETIC

<Ah-set-tik>

Austere; stark; frugal;

Self-denial.

You are ascetic and have great self-control.

A - SCETIC

Scetic	(Reminds)	Skeptic

Memory Trick: A skeptic will not do it.

SET TIC

He lived an ascetic life after being stranded on a desert island.

You espy a snake. It is coming towards you. It has speckles and coral eyes. You don't you run away?

Espy means to see from far away. It is not near you.

FORBEAR

<For-bare>

Avoid; abstain; refrain;

Not doing something on purpose.

I will forbear cookies and I will not eat them anymore.

FOR - BEAR

For	(Reminds)	For
Bear	(Reminds)	Bare

Memory Trick: For it is bare when we do not do it.

FORBARE

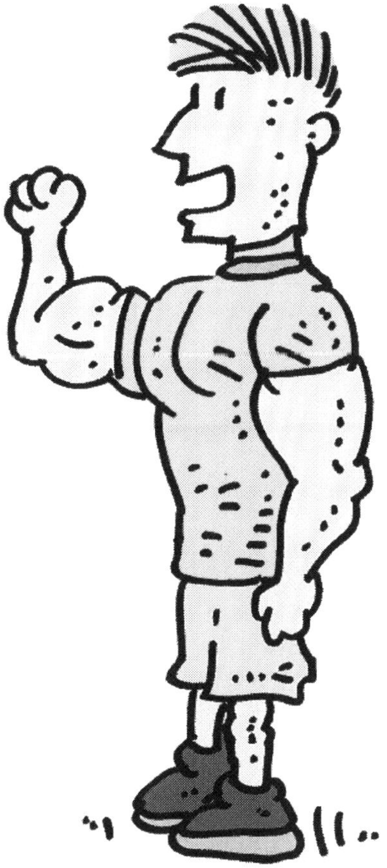

I was out of shape until I decided to forbear junk food.

ESCHEW

<Es-shoo>

Avoid; shun; abandon;

Abstaining by staying away.

I will eschew buying comics because I own too many.

ES - CHEW

Es	(Reminds)	Sss or hiss
Chew	(Rhymes)	Shoo or go away

Memory Trick: Hiss. Shoo! Go away!

SSS SHOO

I will eschew donuts and not eat them again.

Your friend is lonely. You send her a massive missive. She enjoys it again and again. Why does she enjoy it?

You sent her a big letter. A missive is a communication sent by mail. She is enjoying reading it over and over.

SCUTTLEBUTT

<Skud-del-but>

Babble; hearsay; rumor;

Spreading gossip without verifying the truth.

I never talk scuttlebutt because I don't like to spread gossip.

SCUTTLE - BUTT

Scuttle	(Reminds)	Scuttle
Butt	(Reminds)	But

Memory Trick: It is a scuttle and we say, "But".

SCUTTLE BUT

YOU HAVE SCUTTLEBUTT,
AND YOU LET IT SLIP,
WITHOUT KNOWING WHAT,
SO IT'S JUST GOSSIP.

FLUMMOX

<Flum-mux>

Baffle; puzzle; mystify;

Causing confusion or bewilderment.

The puzzles flummox me and I can't solve them.

FLUM - M - OX

Flum	(Reminds)	Flub or mess up
Ox	(Reminds)	Ox or dumb animal

Memory Trick: Flub something like a dumb ox.

FLUB OX

I can always flummox the boy by doing the coin-from-the-ear magic trick.

Q: You go to a laudation and bring clothes. You use suds and torrid water. Why did your clothes not get cleaned?

A: A laudation is a tribute. Someone is praised with a speech at a laudation. No laundry will be washed.

LAMINA

<Lam-in-ah>

Bark; sheet; coat;

Laying down a coating with a thin layer.
The snow laid down a lamina and a white blanket covered everything.

LAM - INA

Lam	(Reminds)	A lamb

Memory Trick: A lamb is covered in white wool.
LAMB

There was a lamina of snow at the top of the mountain.

ASSAIL

<Ah-sale>

Bash; blast; slam;

Attacking violently.

The rain will assail the windows by pounding against them all night.

ASSAIL

Assail	(Reminds)	Assault

Memory Trick: It is an assault when you attack.
ASSAULT

Q: Your friend says his hat is expensive. You say, "Your hat is ignoble." Why does your friend look at you funny?

THE RAIN AND WIND ASSAILS THE WINDOWS.

DIFFIDENT

<Dif-fi-dent>

Bashful; meek; unsure;

Lacking in confidence.

I was a diffident child, but now I am confident.

DIFFI - DENT

Diffi	(Reminds)	Different
Dent	(Reminds)	To dent or damage

Memory Trick: We are different and it dents our confidence

DIFFERENT DENT

A: Ignoble means inferior.

They were both diffident and would not come out to speak with me.

NATATORIUM

<Nah-tah-tore-ee-um>

Bath; tank; pool;

Being a swimming pool or bath.

She was in the natatorium and bathed all day.

NATA - TORIUM

Nata	(Reminds)	Nature
Torium	(Reminds)	Aquarium

Memory Trick: Nature swims in an aquarium.

NATURE AQUARIUM

Q: Your car is stagnant. You push the pedal down. It quickly goes at a vapid pace. What do you probably do next?

A: Get out of the car. Vapid means being lifeless or unanimated. The car is not moving.

We stayed in the natatorium all day.

ESTUARY

<Es-chew-air-re>

Bay; gulf; cove;

Forming a body of water where a river meets the ocean.

We turned in the estuary and went up river.

ESTU - ARY

Estu	(Reminds)	It is to
Ary	(Rhymes)	Airy

Memory Trick: A river runs to the airy bay.

ES TU AIRY

We floated into the estuary, but decided not to go swimming.

NASCENT

<Na-sent>

Beginning; promising; growing

The new start of a thing that will continue on a long time.
The company was nascent when I started and I was the first employee.

N - ASCENT

Ascent	(Reminds)	Ascent or rising up

Memory **Trick:** We begin the ascent by with the first step
ASCENT

Q: You find broccoli to be flocculent. You eat it anyway. A scent wafts from you. Why do I not leave the room?

A sprout, a chick and a new sunrise are examples of nascent beginnings.

CREDENCE

<Kre-dense>

Belief; trust; acceptance

Believing that something is true.

I give credence to the gossip because I believe the rumors.

CRED - ENCE

Cred	(Reminds)	Credible
Ence	(Rhymes)	Sense

Memory Trick: We know it's credible when it makes sense.

CREIDBLE SENSE

A: Flocculent means clumpy like wool. Broccoli is clumpy. The scent is probably perfume.

I do not give any credence to the existence of monsters. Why do you ask?

CASTIGATE

<Cast-ee-gayt>

Berate; lecture; scold;

Criticizing in an angry way.

I will castigate him later and scold him in private.

CAST - T - GATE

Cast	(Reminds)	Cast out
Gate	(Reminds)	Gate

Memory Trick: We cast out and close the gate when we are angry.

CAST GATE

Q: You have a ram in your bunk.

Why do you call it rambunctious?

WHEN YOU CASTIGATE,
YOU CAN BE MEAN,
MAYBE YOU SHOULD WAIT,
AND NOT MAKE A SCENE.

ACERBIC

<Ah-sir-bick>

Bitter; sour; cutting;

Acting unkind in a harsh manner.

You are acerbic when you are being cruel.

ACER - BIC

Acer	(Reminds)	Ace or expert
Bic	(Reminds)	Bicker

Memory Trick: An ace at bickering is a bitter person.

ACE BICKER

A: It is out of control. Rambunctious means loud and out of control.

His acerbic words hurt my feelings.

INFINITESIMAL

<In-fin-ee-tes-ee-mal>

Bitty; teeny; tiny;

Something that is exceptionally small.

It is infinitesimal because we need a microscope to measure it.

INFINITE - SIMAL

Infinite	(Reminds)	Infinite
Simal	(Reminds)	Small

Memory Trick: Being infinite and small.

INFINITE SMALL

Q: You say, "This chocolate cake is dank!" Do you eat it?

He wore an infinitesimal hat on his head. It was too tiny.

REDACT

<Re-dakt>

Black out; obscure; ink out;

Editing out words by blacking them out.

Redact the document and censor the secrets.

RED - ACT

Red	(Reminds)	Red
Act	(Reminds)	Fact

Memory Trick: We red out the facts that they should not see.

RED ACT

A. No. Dank means: being too moist. It is probably too soggy.

WHEN YOU REDACT,
WORDS YOU BLACKED OUT,
YOU CHANGED MY ACT,
NOW THE MEANING IS IN
DOUBT.

EXTOL

<Ex-toll>

Bless; glorify; laud;

Praising a person.

You extol musicians because you love their music.

EX - TOL

Ex	(Reminds)	Ex or the past
Tol	(Reminds)	Toll or result

Memory Trick: I praise you because your ex-toll is good.

EX TOLL

Q: I like to cajole you. What am I doing?

He will always extol about his cat. It must be a great cat.

FAUX PAS

<Fo-pa>

Blunder; error; misstep;

Making a mistake.

It is a faux pas because burping in public is wrong.

FAUX - PAS

Faux	(Reminds)	Fake
Pas	(Reminds)	Pass

Memory Trick: A fake pass we should not have made.

FAKE PASS

A: I am coaxing you. I am using flattery to convince you to do something.

It is a faux pas to wear a clown bowtie to a business meeting.

INTRERPID

<In-trep-pid>

Bold; courageous; valiant;

Exhibiting bravery.

The knight was intrepid when he rode his horse gallantly into battle.

INTREPID

Intrepid	(Reminds)	Intimidate

Memory Trick: We intimidate others when we are brave.

INTIMIDATE

The intrepid mouse kept scaring the cat.

You climb up and addle your horse. You grab the reigns and shout "Tally-ho!" Why don't you go anywhere?

Addle means to confuse. You confused your horse.

TEMERITY

<Tem-mer-rit-tee>

Bold; daring; nerve;

Being foolish and unafraid of danger.

Your temerity won the day because you were brave enough to fight.

TE - MERIT - Y

Merit	(Reminds)	Merit

Memory Trick: You merit praise because you are brave.

MERIT

The mouse showed great temerity when he used the cats as a trampoline.

37456644R00070

Printed in Great Britain
by Amazon